WHEN ARE WE GOING TO GET THERE, MOMMY CROC?

2019 © Penélope Martins, texto
2019 © Camila Teresa, ilustração
2019 © Fábio Meneses, adaptação
2019 © Editora de Cultura
ISBN: 978-85-293-0216-4

Todos os direitos desta edição reservados
EDITORA DE CULTURA LTDA.
Rua Pirajá, 1.117
03190-170 – São Paulo – SP
Fone: (11) 2894-5100
atendimento@editoradecultura.com.br
www.editoradecultura.com.br

Primeira edição: Outubro de 2019
Impressão: 5ª 4ª 3ª 2ª 1ª
Ano: 23 22 21 20 19

CIP-BRASIL. CATALOGAÇÃO NA PUBLICAÇÃO
Sindicato Nacional dos Editores de Livros, RJ

M345f

    Martins, Penelope, 1973-
      When are we going to get there, mommy croc? / Penelope Martins ; ilustração
Camila Teresa ; tradução Fábio Meneses. - 1. ed. - São Paulo : Editora de Cultura, 2019.
      40 p. : il. ; 21 cm.

    Tradução de : Falta muito, mamãe crocodilo?
    ISBN: 978-85-293-0216-4

    1. Poesia. 2. Literatura infantil brasileira. I. Teresa, Camila. II. Meneses, Fábio.
    III. Título. IV. Título: When are we going to get there, Mommy Croc?

CDD: 808.899282
CDU: 82-93(81)

Leandra Felix da Cruz - Bibliotecária - CRB-7/6135

PENÉLOPE MARTINS · CAMILA TERESA

WHEN ARE WE GOING TO GET THERE, MOMMY CROC?

ADAPTED FOR ENGLISH BY FÁBIO MENESES

MOTHER CROC HARVESTED STRAWBERRIES, BLACKBERRIES AND FIGS.
SHE GOES OUT WITH HER KIDS FOR THE SUNDAY TRIP.

THE LITTLE CROCODILES ARE UNEASY AND DISTRESSED,
CANNOT WAIT FOR THE PICNIC AND THE TASTY SNACKS.
SO, THEY ASK ENDLESSLY OUT LOUD TO HER:
MOMMY CROC, WHEN WE'RE GOING TO GET THERE?

MOTHER CROCODILE IS PATIENT, ALWAYS WILLING TO TEACH:
"BAD THINGS COME FAST, GOOD THINGS CAN TAKE LONGER TO REACH."
IT SEEMS THAT SHE IS USUALLY RIGHT,
A COLD COMES QUICKLY, AS FAST AS A FLASHLIGHT!

BUT BIRTHDAY PARTIES, WITH A CAKE AND CANDIES,
THEY TAKE TOO LONG, A FULL YEAR TO ARRIVE...

THE PICNIC BASKET IS ALL SET WITH THEIR FOOD.
OUTSIDE, A RADIANT SUN SHINES OVER THE WOODS.
THE SMALL CROCODILES GET READY FOR ADVENTURE,
CHEWING WITH THEIR BIG MOUTHS A LARGE BITE OF VEGETABLES.

ONE OF THEM WEARS HIS FAVOURITE COAT,
WHILE THE OTHER PREFERS HIS TRUNKS.
ONE CANNOT LIVE WITHOUT HIS RAIN BOOTS,
WHILE ANOTHER GOES BAREFOOT LIKE A MONK.

13

LEAVING HOME, MOTHER CROCODILE LOCKS THE FRONT DOOR.
SHE ALWAYS HIDES THE KEY BETWEEN THE CARPET AND THE FLOOR.

A NICE HAT MOTHER CROC WEARS ON TOP OF HER HEAD,
THAT PROTECTS HER FROM THE STRONG SUN THAT SHINES IN THE SKY AHEAD.
ALL SET, THE JOURNEY OF THE CROC FAMILY IS ABOUT TO START,
A PICNIC ON THE LAKE SIDE, A QUIET SUNDAY GOES BY.

BUT AS SOON AS THEY TAKE THE FIRST STEP OUTSIDE THE COTTAGE,
A SHRILL IS HEARD. ANOTHER THIN VOICE IS HEARD TOO:
"MOMMY CROC, ARE WE CLOSE NOW?
HOW LONG WILL IT TAKE TO GET THERE?"

THE CROCODILE CUBS KEEP ON ASKING THE SAME, AGAIN AND ANEW.
MOTHER CROCODILE, ALWAYS CHEERFUL AND SMILEY,
SHAKES HER TAIL, WAVES HER HAT AND FOLLOWS ON CALMLY.

THEY CLIMB A HILL, GO DOWN THROUGH A PATH SO NARROW,
THEN SEE A WARNING PLATE POINTING
TO THE RIGHT LIKE AN ARROW:

"FASTER PATH TO THE GREAT BLUE LAKE. THE TREE ON THE LEFT,
HEADING TO THE SOUTH" IS THE WAY THEY MUST TAKE.
THE CROCODILE FAMILY SEARCHES FOR THE LITTLE SHORTCUT IN A SPREE.
THEY FOLLOW THE STRAIGHT LINE, PASSING BY THE LARGE OAK TREE.

"YOU BETTER WATCH YOUR STEPS! THE WAY UP IS STEEP"
RECOMMENDS MOTHER CROCODILE TO WATCH FOR THE HEAP.
THEY HAVE CLIMBED UP, THEY HAVE MADE TURNS,
THEY HAVE PAST THE OAK TREE
BUT THE LOVELY LAKE THEY STILL CANNOT SEE...

AND AGAIN,
THE VOICES OF THE CHILDREN ARE HEARD EVERYWHERE:
"MOMMY CROC, WHEN WE'RE GOING TO GET THERE?"

FROM THE NORTH COMES THE STRONG WIND, THAT BLOWS
MOTHER CROCODILE'S HAT AWAY.
SITTING ON A WALNUT BRANCH, LORD SQUIRREL SAYS:
"THAT WIND STARTED YESTERDAY;
UNTIL TOMORROW IT SHALL STAY!

BETTER KEEP SOME NUTS AND HAZELNUTS IN MY BURROW".
"MISTER SQUIRREL, IS THIS THE CORRECT WAY TO THE BLUE LAKE?
PLEASE LET ME KNOW"
MOTHER CROCODILE POINTS THE PATH HEADING SOUTH.

LITTLE CROCODILES CAN NO LONGER CONTROL
THE IMMENSE DESIRE TO ASK MOMMY ONCE AGAIN...
BUT LOOKING AT MOTHER, WHO SEEMS ANNOYED AND UPSET,
THEY DECIDE TO WALK SINGING AN OLD SONG TO DE-STRESS:

"MY HAT, IT HAS THREE CORNERS, THREE CORNERS HAS MY HAT, AND HAD IT NOT THREE CORNERS, IT WOULD NOT BE MY HAT."

THEY FOLLOW IN LINE, MOMMY AND HER LITTLE CHILDREN,
SINGING, THEY HIGHLIGHT THE SCENERY ALONG THE WAY.
LONG TAILS ON SUCH SHORT PAWS,
MAKES THE CROCS AN ARCHITECTURE TO PORTRAY

ONCE THEY FORGET THE DELAY, THEY TOSS THEIR TAILS ALONG THE WAY.
BACK IN THE GOOD MOOD, THE TRIP FLOWS AWAY.

ALWAYS LUCKY, THEY FOUND ANOTHER WARNING PLATE!
ADJUSTING HER GLASSES, MOTHER CROCODILE CHECKS WHAT IT STATES.

BEST WAY TO THE BLUE LAKE, STRAIGH
JUST FOLLOW THE ELBOW TRACK TO THE E

"BEST WAY TO THE BLUE LAKE, STRAIGHT AWAY,
JUST FOLLOW THE ELBOW TRACK TO THE EAST".
BUT IT SEEMS THE PUPPIES ARE TIRED OF WALKING ANYWHERE.
"MOMMY CROC, WHEN WE'RE GOING TO GET THERE?"

THE ZIGZAG TRAIL RESERVES A NICE SURPRISE,
RASPBERRY BUSH STUFFED WITH FLAVOUR
MOTHER CROCODILE TASTES FIRST, THE PUPPIES EAT AND THEN SIGH
THEY CHEW MANY SWEET THINGS, FILLING THEIR BELLIES HARD AS ARMOURS!

A WELL-DESERVED PAUSE, WITH SUCH JUICY AND FRESH BERRY,
BRING BACK THEIR JOY, INCREASE THEIR ENERGY!

ALTHOUGH WELL FED, THE SMALL CROCS SAY THEIR LOUD RHYME:
"MOTHER CROC, HOW LONG ARE WE FROM OUR DIVING TIME?"

THE SUN COMES FROM THE EAST, SETS ON THE WEST,
DAY AFTER DAY IT FLOWS.
THE COMPASS INDICATES THE GREAT LAKE AMONG THE MEADOWS.
THE LOUD QUACKS ANNOUNCE, MALLARDS,
SWANS AND DUCKS SINGING THEIR CORNETS,
AND PRETTY SOON, THE LITTLE CROCS WILL ALL BE SOAK AND WET.

MOM SETS THE PICNIC: TOWEL UNDERNEATH AND BASKET ON TOP.
AFTER THE PARTY, THE CROC CUBS WILL MUNCH ALL THE FOOD, GUESS WHAT!

INSIDE THE LAKE, CROCODILES SWIM WITH THE DUCKS TO FRESHEN-UP,
OUT OF THE WATER, CROCODILES AND MALLARDS PLAY AND CATCH UP.
EVERYONE IS A FRIEND AND TOGETHER LAUGH IN UPROAR,
JOKING WITH THE SWANS, IMITATING THEIR NECKS STRETCHED,
THE WAY THEY ADORE.

WHAT A DAY WELL SPENT, THIS SUNDAY AT THE LAKE.
EVERYONE HAD A GOOD TIME SINCE DAYBREAK!
NOW IT'S LATE, ALWAYS TICKING IS THE CLOCK.
THE LITTLE HOUSE IS FAR, NOW IT'S TIME TO WALK.
BUT AS SOON AS THEY FOLLOW THEIR TRAIL BACK HOME,
THEY CANNOT BARE
THE CHILDREN SHOUT AGAIN:

"MOMMY CROC, WHEN WE'RE GOING TO GET THERE?"

THIS BOOK IS A TRIBUTE TO JAMES BARRIE,
PETER PAN'S FATHER, NOT TO MENTION
THE IMMENSE TIC-TAC CROCODILE...

HI, MY NAME IS CAMILA TERESA, I'M AN ILLUSTRATOR AND DESIGNER. I LIKE CUTE DUCKLINGS IN THE CALM LAKE, BUT I'M AFRAID OF CROCODILE BITES. I AM GLAD I COULD DRAW THE CROCS VERY NICELY.

HELLO, MY NAME IS PENELOPE MARTINS, I REALLY LIKE TO WRITE STORIES, SOME VERY QUICK AND OTHERS WITH ENOUGH TIME TO WRITE. IF I WERE IN MOTHER CROCO'S SHOES, HEARING SO MUCH FROM HER PUPPIES, I WOULD HAVE HAD A HISSY FIT.

HELLO, MY NAME IS FABIO MENESES, I REALLY LIKE TO THINK STORIES IN DIFFERENT LANGUAGES, SO I ADAPTED THE TEXT FROM PORTUGUESE TO ENGLISH. HOW ABOUT YOU, CAN YOU SPEAK ANOTHER LANGUAGE, LIKE FRENCH, PORTUGUESE OR JAPANESE?